Contents

Where to Start

The Early Years

Growing Up

Owning Your Life

Tips for Everyday

A little bit about . . . Bonni Greiner

I was raised in a loving Jewish home and became a Christian as an adult shortly before I was married. Reading through the New Testament for the first time proved to be quite confusing for me. There were many verses that I just did not understand. Titus 2:3-5 proved to be three of those verses.

"Likewise, teach the older women to be reverent
in the way they live, not to be slanderers or addicted to
too much wine, but to teach what is good.
Then they can train the younger women to love their
husbands and children, to be self-controlled and pure,
to be busy at home, to be kind, and to be
subject to their husbands, so that no one
will malign the word of God."
Titus 2:3-5

The phrase that I struggled with the most in those verses was to "train the younger women to love their husbands and children." Why did they need to be trained? Didn't all those beautiful feelings of love and devotion come naturally?

Our first year of marriage proved to be quite difficult. I was a Jewish girl raised in the metropolitan Philadelphia area who was now married to a hog farmer residing in a rural country setting, 85 miles away from my childhood home, friends and family. We had a lot of learning and compromising to do.

In five years we added four sons to our family. Now I was beginning to understand Titus 2. I needed an older woman to train me.

Needing an older woman and finding one who was willing to train me were two very different things. The women I asked said that they felt inadequate or were too busy to help me. I turned instead to radio programs like Focus on the Family and read as many books as I could about marriage and motherhood.

God proved to be very faithful in my life, and I gained the confidence and tidbits of wisdom needed to be the wife and mom that He created me to be. I continue to learn daily and thought I would share some tips from my journey that have made being a wife and mother easier and more rewarding.

One of my goals is to live each day without regretting how I spent the time given to me by God. The tips that I share help me to do just that. I pray that this book will be a blessing to you in the spirit of Titus 2.

A little bit about . . . Kathy McClure

I was raised in a loving, Christian home near Lancaster, Pennsylvania. I met my husband later in life and we then had three children in our first four years of marriage. We struggled with some of the same things Bonni shares about in this book, and our desire is to help you find an easier way too!

Reflecting on my early years of parenting, I loved having a baby to cuddle and sing to, but I thought my primary role was to feed him, care for him and keep him alive. Which it, of course, was . . . but thank God that he brought Bonni into my life and challenged me in a new way to consider biblical motherhood.

Through her talks, books and blog, she challenged me to mother in new ways, and it was like having a Titus 2 mom right there with me: talking to me, helping me think through situations, and offering advice. Her insight has been invaluable to me in my journey, as she has helped me to plan ahead and prepare for each new stage, and as she has helped my husband and I rethink some of our parenting approaches.

My prayer is that every mom who reads this book finds the joy that comes from engaging with their children, practicing patience, interacting with them, learning about God and life with them, and being intentional in sharing their spiritual journey with them.

Enjoy the tips in this book and all the real-life examples Bonni shares! You will be blessed.

Faith sees the invisible, believes the unbelievable,
and receives the impossible.

CORRIE TEN BOOM

Building a Foundation

When our children are young and we are needed 24/7, we often feel physically and emotionally drained. Although we will always be moms, our days will not continue to be as full and tiring as they are now. It is hard to imagine, but it is true. The day will come when our children leave our home. What will we have hoped to accomplish? What are our goals as a parent?

My most important goal was to build a strong foundation of faith in my children. I knew that there would be a limited amount of time that they were under my care. I also knew that the world is not always a friendly place. There are no guarantees with our children. They are not puppets. I can only do the best that I can by building a foundation and hope and pray that they make good choices.

"For what shall it profit a man, if he shall gain the whole
world, and lose his own soul?"
Mark 8:36 ESV

There's an easier way.

Here are some tips that made building a foundation of
faith easier for me:

**1. Help them understand that their conception and
birth were part of God's plan.** It was not just luck or a
random act or happenstance. They have a distinct reason
for living. They were chosen.

"For You made the parts inside me.
You put me together inside my mother."
Psalm 139:13 New Life Version (NLV)

"You were chosen by God the Father long ago.
He knew you were to become His children.
You were set apart for holy living by the Holy Spirit. May
you obey Jesus Christ and
be made clean by His blood. May you be full
of His loving-favor and peace."
1 Peter 1:2 New Life Version (NLV)

**Our children were planned and knit
together by a loving God. It was determined that they were to be born.**

2. Teach the children that where they were born and the family in which they were placed is also a part of God's plan.

"He made from one blood
all nations who live on the earth.
He set the times and places where they should live."
Acts 17:26 New Life Version (NLV)

> **They were appointed
> to be in their home.**

3. Try to determine each child's gifting(s). Pray over them and for them regularly. As you start to see their strengths, encourage them in that gifting. Remind them that they are special in God's sight.

> **He knit them together
> with special abilities and
> likes and dislikes because
> they are one of a kind.
> No one can take their place
> in their immediate family
> or in the family of God.**

**4. Spend one on one time with children through-
out the day to intentionally connect with them,** heart
to heart. Join them on the floor to play or read a book or
just snuggle. Even ten minutes of quality time spent one
on one is valuable. Ask them age-related questions: "Do
you know how much God loves you?" "What made you
happy today?" "If you could live today all over again, what
would you like to do again?"

Questions like that expose their heart.

> **It becomes much easier
> to pray for them when we know how
> they currently perceive life.**

5. Be your child's biggest cheerleader. Affirm them
as they demonstrate godly character traits. Have a list of
traits from which you can easily refer. Look for ways to
encourage them in their faith.

We call our home "Base Camp" and we call our family a team. We work together, grow together, succeed and
fail together. We love and support each other, no matter
what.

> **It helps to build a strong foundation.**

* Family rules
Poster

6. **Talk about God a lot.** Have meaningful devotions.

> [4]"Hear, O Israel! The Lord our God is one Lord! [5]And you must love the Lord your God with all your heart and with all your soul and with all your strength. [6]Keep these words in your heart that I am telling you today. [7]Do your best to teach them to your children. Talk about them when you sit in your house and when you walk on the road and when you lie down and when you get up. [8]Tie them as something special to see on your hand and on your forehead. [9]Write them beside the door of your house and on your gates. *Deuteronomy 6:4-8 NLV*

7. **Pray, pray, pray.** Our prayers are powerful and effective, and they have no expiration date. Pray that your children will accept Jesus as their Savior and that they will fulfill the destinies for which they were created. Pray for wisdom in guiding and leading them.

**Wisdom for parenting
is just a prayer away.**

*Love begins by taking care
of the closest ones—the ones at home.*

MOTHER TERESA

A Successful Day

My mom died unexpectedly ten years ago. Although she lived more than 70 years and was able to meet all of her grandchildren, I wasn't ready to 'lose' her. Life as a busy wife and mom suddenly became even harder for me, knowing that I could never again communicate with my mother about our family and life in general. I prayed for someone to come into my life as a mother figure and God, answered by bringing me a Christian woman named Mary. We had a wonderful relationship until she, also, passed away unexpectedly a few years ago.

Several months after her funeral, while eating lunch alone at a restaurant where Mary and I had often eaten together, I broke out in tears and was inconsolable. *What was wrong with me? Why was I so sad?* I had lost other friends and family, but my grief over losing my two 'moms' was so much worse.

I concluded that the reason my grief was almost over-bearing was simply because of love. Mary loved well. My mother loved well. Nothing that this world had to offer was as important to my mother or to Mary as developing deep and strong relationships.

Being together was all that was needed for Mary and me to have a good time. I felt loved. I felt accepted just as I was. Both of the women loved me unconditionally.

That's the kind of mom I want to be. I want to be intentional about loving and accepting people uncondi-tionally.

I want to love well.

If I can do that, I will have lived a successful life. If I can do that today, I will consider it a successful day.

There's an easier way.

Here are some tips:

1. **Make a list of all the things that you love most about YOUR mother's character** and the way that you were raised. Incorporate the items on your list into your life and parenting techniques.

2. **Define success for your life.** What would it look like? Should any changes be made in your daily routine?

3. **Love unconditionally.** Determine if your love has strings attached. Does your love include manipulation, fits of anger, bribery or guilt? If so, be intentional about making changes.

4. **Ask you children if they have a suggestion to help you be a better mom.** You might be surprised!

Practice is the hardest part of learning,
and training is the essence of transformation.

ANN VOSKAMP

Creating Successful Routines

When I get ready for bed each evening, and I look at what was accomplished that day, I want to be able to call it successful. Because life and busyness have a way of taking control of the day, I decided I had better start implementing schedules so that my priorities and goals were accomplished.

After several attempts at scheduling my days, I concluded that schedules were not for me. I knew that schedules work for some moms, but rarely for moms of very young children.

Instead, I implemented routines.

There's an easier way.

Here are some tips:

1. **Give up the fantasy of a perfectly planned and executed day when you have young children.** It may happen, and when it does, it is glorious. When it does not happen—do not feel badly, blame yourself, or assume that every other mom could do a better job. *You are the best mom for your children!*

2. **Moms have a long and extensive job description, but it does not include controlling or fixing everything that might come up in our day.** When something happens that threatens to disrupt your to-do list, quickly and joyfully adjust.

3. **Work around YOUR time schedule.** I LOVE waking up before 6:00 AM and waking my children by 6:30 AM to get an early start. That works for me. What time frame would work for you?

4. **Find a timeframe or plan that fits your personality.** Determine how best to accomplish what is most important to you. I try to achieve my most important goals before lunch. Then if the rest of the day implodes, I feel more relaxed and able to handle it.

5. **Snatch time.** *That's what I call grabbing minutes between other activities to get things done.* It only takes several minutes to quickly fill the dishwasher, or scrub the bathroom sink, or throw laundry in the washer, or send an email, or any number of things. Most of my hope-to-

do list is accomplished when I snatch time between all of the things screaming my name.

6. **Plan daily to have one-on-one time with your children.** There were many nights that I cried myself to sleep because I could not remember if I had kissed and hugged each of my children that day. I had been SO busy doing what seemed to be crucial, that I neglected the most important.

To remedy that, each day before lunch, before nap-time, and before bedtime I hugged, kissed, and played with each of the children.

7. **Claim a verse (or verses) from the Bible upon which to meditate.** I write the verse on a post-it note and place it at my kitchen sink. Thinking about God's word helps remind me of how God wants me to live, and therefore prioritize accordingly.

My favorite verses to meditate on are:

"Be joyful always;
pray continually;
give thanks in all circumstances
for this is God's will for you
in Christ Jesus."
1 Thessalonians 5:16-18 NIV

*God's ultimate goal for your life on earth
is not comfort but character development.
He wants you to grow up spiritually
and become like Christ.*

RICK WARREN

Setting and Achieving Goals

S ometimes we are so busy as moms we feel like we are on autopilot. We attend to the needs of every child, and travel from room to room completing necessary tasks, and then we circle round and round and repeat. My goal when my children were young was to just survive the day with my sanity intact.

Setting attainable goals in the midst of my hectic days can actually improve my mood and my outlook.

There's an easier way.

Here are some tips:

1. **During this season of life, make the goals attainable.** Big, lofty goals can wait until there is more time available

to meet them head on. Examples of lofty goals that would have frustrated and depressed me would have been trying to write a book, start a blog, or run a home business. What would be some examples of lofty goals for you?

2. **Goals should bring you joy.** What would bring you GREAT joy? Reading a book? Getting a manicure? Going to a coffee shop alone for an evening? Meeting a friend for coffee? Organizing your closet? Painting a room? Learning to knit?

Some examples of my goals were: creating time to spend one-on-one with each of my children every day, reading thirty minutes a day, and exercising with a DVD three times a week. These were realistic goals that brought me great joy and satisfaction.

3. **Have some daily goals that will bring you joy and have eternal value.** Two of my favorites were praying for each of my family members and affirming each of my children every day. My goal was to accomplish those every day by lunch time. By connecting it to lunch time there was less of a chance for me to forget.

I also savored time alone with God—having devotions and asking directions for my day. Even 2 to 5 minutes alone with God will set the tone for your entire day.

4. **Goal backwards.** When you go to bed tonight, what will you have hoped to accomplish so that you would consider the day to be a success? List those things in the morning and make them a priority.

5. **Try not to be too disappointed or hard on yourself.** Sometimes, and more often than we'd like, the day has a way of turning out a lot differently than we had hoped or expected. Our goals may not be met. Life has ups and downs, and we are smart to roll with them.

I have come to realize that my Plan A may not be God's Plan A, but His plan is always for my benefit and ultimate good.

Potty Training

J was blessed to have visitors one weekend who had two sons a little older than my firstborn. They suggested that I potty train my 22-month-old son with their help. I agreed and within three days he was trained. I used the same system with my next seven children, all with similar success.

There's an easier way.

Here are some tips:

1. **Know that EVERYONE, eventually, will be potty trained.** Unless there is a severe medical problem, your child will NOT be the first teenager who is not potty trained.

2. **Be patient.** There are many theories and systems describing the best ways to potty train children, but they ALL require patience. Try to remind yourself to relax, and

'shake it off' if the child has accidents. Accidents WILL happen and may even occur for several months. They have NOT had to think about using a potty for their entire life until this point, so be patient.

3. **Evaluate the child's readiness.** Have they shown an interest in using the potty? Do they seem to understand the process at all? My eight children were between 22 and 25 months old when they were potty trained. Many boys, in particular, could be 2 1/2 to 3 years old before they can successfully be potty trained. Potty training is an area of our children's lives that we cannot force or regulate. Do not make it a battleground. We, as parents, will lose.

4. **Make life as easy as possible during this process.** Use Pull-Ups for naps and overnight, as accidents will most likely happen. It saves on laundry duty and is much better than waking the child every hour or so to take them to the bathroom as many people suggest. I have never heard of one success story using that method. A mom's sleep is a precious commodity.

5. **Pray for wisdom, and don't be too embarrassed to ask friends for advice and support.** You may try several systems before you have success with a child, and what worked with one child may not work for a sibling.

6. **If you'd like to try my system,** you can find my video on YouTube: Potty Training in 3 Days by Bonni Greiner.

Complaining is dangerous business.
It can damage or even destroy
your relationship with God,
your relationships with other people,
and even your relationship with yourself.

JOYCE MEYER

No Whining

As hard as it was to lose sleep while raising young children, it was probably even more difficult for me to continually be aware of their need for training. *I knew that training my children was a necessity, and I knew that as their mom, I was the best person to do it.* Part of that training involved helping the children learn to communicate. Philippians 2:14 became a key verse, "do everything without complaining or arguing." **I added the word whining.**

I understand that very young children can not verbalize what they are feeling. When they make sounds like whining, they are usually just trying to get our attention because they need some help. However, when an 18-month-old or two or three-year-old start whining, they are old enough to learn to communicate instead.

Whining is annoying, frustrating, and often used to manipulate us. They whine when they know that what they are asking is usually going to receive a 'no' answer. It is a pretty smart tactic on their part because what parent has not felt like giving in after a child whines repeatedly?!

I think that we are doing a disservice to our children if we allow them to whine. I found it is easy to stop the whining by *teaching them how to express themselves in an acceptable manner instead.*

Our children want to please us.

There's an easier way.

Here are some tips:

1. **When a child starts to whine, immediately approach them and tell them that we do not whine.** Explain that you are excited to hear what they have to say, but you will not listen to whining.

Role-play with the child. Use a happy voice to repeat what the child just said to you. Ask them to repeat it with their happy voice. If they obey, hug and kiss them. If they don't obey, have them repeat it again. Explain again how important it is to communicate nicely and not whine. Do not give in to their whining. Tell them that you will listen to them as soon as they use their happy voice.

My motto is, "If you choose to whine, my answer will be no."

2. **Sometimes our children whine to get our attention.** Maybe they just need some more of you. Cuddle

with them, play with them, show them a lot of physical affection and attention. You may have to be more intentional about the amount of time you spend with each child. I tried my best to spend at least 10-15 minutes with each child before lunch, before nap time, before supper and before bedtime. It did not always happen, but that was my goal.

3. **I noticed that often my children would whine about something that they didn't understand.** For instance, if I told them we were going to go to the playground tomorrow, they would keep whining and whining and asking when we were leaving. I learned it was not a good idea to talk to my children about things that would be happening in the future. Young children don't understand the concept of time.

4. **Pray for wisdom to know the best way to deal with each of your children.** As elementary as it sounds, prayer is our most powerful and effective tool in raising our children. The God who knit our children together and who knows their every thought has promised to give us wisdom if we ask. He loves them more than we could ever imagine.

Every 60 seconds you spend upset,
is a minute of happiness you'll never get back.

UNKNOWN

Cheerful Workers

"Whatever you do, work at it with all your heart,
as working for the Lord, not for men. Since you know
that you will receive an inheritance from the Lord
as a reward. It is the Lord Christ you are serving."
Colossians 3:23-24

This became a foundational scripture for our family. There were so many chores that needed to be done in our home every day. I needed help. My husband suggested that I become a very efficient manager and teach the children to do chores that would make my load easier.

I found that there were several advantages to teaching my children how to work, in addition to the obvious one. I also noticed very quickly, however, that a cheerful worker did a much better job at their task than a child who was grumbling or complaining or working without any enthusiasm. With a little effort and work on my part, it did not take long to help my children learn to be cheerful workers and to enjoy learning new tasks and ways to help me around the house and our farm.

There's an easier way.

Here are some tips:

1. **Teach your children how to get things done and help with chores.** I found these benefits to be true:
   - It helped them to feel like an *important* and significant part of our family.
   - It helped them to have *confidence* in their ability to learn new things.
   - It helped them learn the benefits of *working hard* and making the best use of their time.

2. **Memorize verses** like Proverbs 17:22, "A cheerful heart is good medicine, but a crushed spirit dries up the bones." Role-play what it looks like to be a happy worker, as opposed to one who is reluctantly getting things done.

MAKE IT FUN!
Try doing chores while singing
"A Joyful Heart is Good Medicine" from
Steve Green's *Hide 'Em In Your Heart Volume 2.*

3. **Be a good role model.** How do you act, and what do you say when you are getting your work done? Do you act irritated? I found that it helped my attitude to put some praise music on the CD player and sing as I worked. The children would sing along with me, and before we knew it, we were laughing and working together like a well-oiled machine.

4. **Talk about Colossians 3:23-24 when you work.**
- Explain what it means to work with all of our hearts, as working for God and not for man.
- Explain what it means to receive an inheritance as a reward from God.
- Explain what it means to serve the Lord Jesus. What does that look like in our life? How can we serve Him? *Everything that we do to help others, is serving Jesus.*
- Ask your children for examples of what they have done to help others or to help their siblings, or what they plan to do to help others.

5. **Talk to your children about time.** When we say we are wasting time, whose time are we wasting? Do we have any control over the amount of time that we live? Can we increase the amount of time in our day by even thirty seconds? No. *God owns time.* So, when we are wasting time, we are wasting His time. We don't want to do that. *Time is a precious gift.*

6. **Affirm your children as you see them working cheerfully.** Affirm their character, even more than their performance.

It does not take long at all before children work cheerfully because they see the results in doing things well, quickly, and with a good attitude.

꿍 ၆ 꿈

Teachable Moments

My firstborn was a perfectly happy baby during the day, but at night he screamed every hour or hour and a half. This went on for months. I decided to try to make the most of the frequent times spent trying to soothe him by talking to him. I whispered how much I loved him, how important he was to God and to us, how he would grow up to be strong and courageous, and on and on.

As hard as those months were I would not have traded them for more sleep because **I learned the value of speaking into my children's lives.**

Training up our children in the way they should go can be accomplished little by little through teachable moments.

There's an easier way.

Here are some tips:

1. 'Catch' your child being good. Look for behavior displaying a godly character trait, and affirm them. For example, if my three-year-old gently touches her little brother's face to calm him down, I would say, "Sally, that was so loving and kind."

2. Use behavior that does not please you to also become a teachable moment. If I see Jack, my two year old, trying to kick the family dog, I would quickly pick up the toddler, and create a teachable moment. "Jack, members of our family do not hurt animals or people. We show kindness at all times." *(Of course, if the behavior continues, it becomes willful disobedience, and I would discipline him.)*

3. Look at your children with eyes of approval and love. They can read our body language. If our words do not match our body language, we are giving mixed signals.

4. When you want to make an impact, speak to your child, eye to eye. Either lift them up, or kneel down to their level.

5. Welcome them home with open arms and enthusiasm. When you are reunited with your child after a play date, preschool class, or any outing, show excitement both by word and body language. It is a wonderful way to show them how much they are valued and loved.

*Is prayer your steering wheel
or your spare tire?*
CORRIE TEN BOOM

Find the Humor

ife as a busy mom of four young sons in five years got to be too much. I felt like my life was out of control, and I was not having fun. I projected that because life was this hard now, it would continue to be this hard for the next 5, 10 or maybe 15 years. I came to the conclusion that I would never have fun again. It sounds ridiculous now, but for those of you living in the trenches of raising young children, you can probably see how I would feel that way. We have so much to do every day and what we do gets undone many times over.

With God's help, I came to the conclusion that my life would remain busy, so *it became my choice as to whether I would have an attitude of gratitude and thankfulness or one filled with complaining and feeling resentful.*

I chose to start finding humor in my day. As I changed my attitude, I began to realize that many of the same situations and activities that had caused me to feel stressed and angry could cause me to laugh. It was all in my attitude.

As time went on, it became easier and easier to find humor in the very same things that would have previously caused me to become upset. Life is just too short. I did not want to look back on my life and wish that I had enjoyed my children more than I did. Over time, I discovered that there were four general categories that were robbing me of my joy. I call them the *fun robbers*.

There's an easier way.

Here are some tips:

1. **Children act childish.** Accidents happen. Joyfully, children seem to have more of them than adults which means that as they get older there will be fewer and fewer of them. When children cause unexpected, hard things, in our life, we can still choose to find humor in the situation. Here are three examples of potential fun robbers that have occurred in our house.

One day when I was busy doing mommy things around the house, it occurred to me that I hadn't heard or seen my two-year-old or three-year-old daughters in several minutes. That's never a good thing. When I finally found them, something about their appearance alarmed me. I realized that they were both missing their bangs. My three-year-old daughter had decided to cut her sister's bangs and unfortunately did a very bad job. There was just a little, jagged row of extremely short hair. She must have then decided to cut her own bangs, and although they were very jagged, at least they were a half inch to an inch long. Their appearance alone could've easily prompted me to have a mommy tantrum, but what made it even worse was that the very next day, we had an appointment as a family to have our annual Christmas card picture taken. I had an option. I had a choice. *I chose to laugh.* The whole scenario was unbelievable. The Christmas picture taken the next day has become one of our favorites.

Another example involves one of my sons. One day my second oldest son decided to bring his heavy set of barbells up from the basement to the kitchen to show me how strong he was. The only problem was, on that particular day, it did not go well, and he dropped the heavy barbells on our kitchen floor, breaking the floor. I had a choice. My son didn't mean to break the floor. I had never thought to warn him not to drop heavy barbells on the floor. *I chose to laugh.* Our kitchen floor still bears some of the marks from that day.

The third example involves our dog. One of my young daughters purchased an absolutely adorable Poodle/ Bichon puppy. It was almost all white except for a few patches of peach colored fur. One day I walked into the kitchen to find a dog that resembled ours, but had orange and blue stripes. Two of my daughters had used vegetable dye and painted the dog. Why had it never occurred to me to warn the children not to paint our dog??? I couldn't discipline them for willful disobedience, *so I laughed.* What good would it have done to yell and scream? I figured it would grow out in time, which it did.

2. **Another *fun robber* is the dangerous practice called comparison.** It is not a good idea to compare our husbands with other husbands, or our children with other children, or our lives with anyone else's life. It is easy to look at another family and think how much happier they look, or how much more attentive the husband seems to be than your husband, or how well-behaved the children are compared to yours. But the point is—we really don't know what their life is like. And even if they are the perfect family—whatever that means—it is not our family. God commands us not to envy or want what our neighbor has. *Comparison and envy rob us of the joy that God intends for us to have.*

3. **Accept help.** There were many times when I was struggling with my young children, and a neighbor or a friend offered to bring a meal or to help me to clean or to babysit my children. Unfortunately, my pride got in the way, and I refused the help. I guess I wanted them to think that I could handle everything myself. I should have accepted help. Not only was I denying myself the help I desperately needed, but I was robbing them of the blessing that they would have received from sowing into my life.

One dear friend ignored my continual refusal of her help. She dropped off a huge pan of frozen lasagna at my front door and informed me that it was up to me what happened to it. I could let it rot there, or I could bring it in and serve it to my family or freeze it for a better time. The choice was mine. What a special friend!

4. **Trying too hard to be a better mom can be a *fun robber.*** What exactly is a better mom? Who is a better mom? Often, we can't define it, and yet we strive to be one. Would we know one if we found her? We can often be our own worst enemy. We can heap so much condemnation on ourself that we lose our joy.

Instead, let's try to improve as a Christian. Let's ask God to help us walk in faith, trusting Him. Let's ask God to give us the wisdom that we need when we need it. Let's ask Him for grace daily and thank Him for his mercy. We can ask Him to help us exhibit the fruit of the Spirit more and more each day.

The more we allow God control and guidance in our lives, the more joy and fun we will have. Each day I try to remember to pray and ask God to help me love my children the way He loves them and help me see my children the way that He sees them.

Every decision you need to make,
every task you need to accomplish,
every relationship you need to navigate,
every element of daily life you need to traverse,
God has already perfectly matched up with an equivalent to
overflowing supply of His grace.
PRISCILLA SHIRER

Discipline

O ur children need boundaries. The Bible clearly states that we are to train our children.

"Train up a child in the way he should go,
And when he is old he will not depart from it."
Proverbs 22:6 (NKJV)

Like so many other areas of parenting, there are not practice sessions for training our children. It is entirely on the job training, without a detailed order of events or how-to manual. To make it even more unsettling and difficult, asking ten people for advice will probably result in ten very different opinions.

There's an easier way.
Here are some tips:

1. **Simplify the discipline process.** Determine and define what behavior is acceptable and unacceptable. My hubby and I came up with six non-negotiables. If our child was being willfully disobedient in any of these six areas, we would talk to him about his behavior, and if the misbehavior continued, we would discipline him. The form of discipline varied with the child and the circumstances.

6 Non-Negotiables

1. We do not hurt anyone, or any living thing, with our words or through our actions. *(1 John 3:18)*
2. We are thankful in all things. *(1Thessalonians 5:16-18)*
3. We were born to be a witness for Jesus at all times. *(Matthew 24:14)*
4. We do not complain or argue. We learn to communicate what we are feeling. *(Phil. 2:14)*
5. We honor and obey our parents. *(Ephesians. 6:2)*
6. We learn to be content. *(Philippians 4:11)*

2. **Don't discipline in anger.** Do what needs to be done to calm down before administering discipline. The child can misconstrue anger as rejection or even repulsion. We want to learn to look at our children the way that God looks at us. He loves the sinner but hates the sin. The child must understand that he will always be loved unconditionally, but we as his parents are responsible for helping to equip him to fulfill his destiny in Christ.

3. **Pick your battles.** If a child isn't breaking a non-negotiable, it may not be a disciplinary offense. Decide if the act is an act of willful disobedience, or just childish foolishness.

4. **It is important to role play.** Many times our children know what is wrong, but they don't know the right way to handle a situation. Role-playing helps them know how to act appropriately.

God doesn't look at how much we do,
but with how much love we do it.
MOTHER TERESA

Discipline with Grace

J t is up to us as parents to train our children. How does God look at the disobedience of our children? Is He embarrassed? No, I don't think so. When our children choose to sin, it is an indication that correction is needed. It is as simple as that.

"While we were still sinners,
Christ died for us."
Romans 5:8

He loves our children unconditionally, but not their sins. We need to love them unconditionally also, but deal with willful disobedience. We need them to know that we will always love them and accept them just as they are because that is grace. It is our responsibility to teach them the importance of obedience and doing what is right. If they willfully disobey, we need to discipline them. Our love for them does not change. Love the sinner, hate the sin.

How do we discipline our children with grace?

There's an easier way.

Here are some tips:

1. **Always look for the positive** in your children. Be intentional about it. Affirm them.

2. **Take the time to think about your actions** as you deal with your children. Are you walking in grace? We misrepresent God to our children when we lack grace.

3. **Do not use manipulation, fear or bribery** to try to coerce your children to change. Change should come about because of a desire to do what is right because it is right. Fear, bribes and manipulation do not change human hearts.

4. **Try not to show favoritism** to one child who may be more compliant and easier to parent than another child.

5. **Yelling is not OK.** If you are angry, step back, relax, and deal with your anger before you deal with your child.

6. **Be consistent and show respect.** Your child needs to know that the boundaries do not change. They need consistency in how you relate to them.

That is grace.

7. **If you are weary or discouraged, ask God to help you.** Wisdom, strength, grace and mercy were paid for along with our salvation at the cross. They are available as we need them, when we ask.

8. **We need to be role models to our children.** We need to choose to walk with grace and joy, and be thankful even in the midst of a struggle or hardship.

We could never learn to be brave and patient,
if there was only joy in the world.
HELEN KELLER

Building Courage in Our Children

J t is important to teach our children about godly character. To affirm them when they demonstrate godly characteristics, such as faithfulness, joy, patience, being content, being diligent, or any other godly character trait. But there is one characteristic, courage, which is different than the rest.

Most of the godly character traits come from within the child as a choice of their will. They can choose to be diligent. They can choose to be joyful or helpful or honest.

But being courageous comes from relying on God's power. It is important that we teach our children the steps to take to become courageous. There are many examples of courage being demonstrated in the Bible. My favorite example to use with my children is the story of David.

When David was chosen as a last resort to conquer Goliath, he stated that it should not be a problem at all because he had already conquered the lion and the bear with God's help. He had a history with God. We need to remind our children that they also have a history with God. Whether they know it or not, God has never forsaken them, or left them alone.

There's an easier way.

Here are some tips:

1. Read them stories about courageous Christians in the Bible. Consider also reading stories of Christian heroes throughout time. An excellent resource for these stories is the "Hero Tales: A Family Treasury of True Stories from the Lives of Christian Heroes" book series.

2. Memorize verses from the Bible that talk about being strong and courageous. Some of our favorites were:

"Be strong in the Lord and in His mighty power."
Ephesians 6:10

"Be strong and courageous, do not be afraid."
Joshua 1:9

"Be on your guard, stand firm in your faith. Be a man of courage. Be strong. Do everything in love."
1 Corinthians 16:13-14

3. Explain that the courage we need comes from God working in us. The Bible describes us as clay pots. Clay pots are fragile, they crack and break very easily. But the Bible explains that God's power lives in us and is working in us. When we need courage, we simply need to ask God to be strong and courageous in us and through us. God never fails.

"We have this treasure in jars of clay
to show this all powerful strength and power
is from God and not from us."
2 Corinthians 4:7

4. Pray with your children when they are about to embark on a new adventure or something that they are nervous about. Ask God to give them the courage that they need. Remind them that God has never let them down, and just as David took care of Goliath, God will give them the courage for their 'giant'.

One of my sons struggled with wetting the bed long after he was potty trained. He refused to go to sleepovers because of the possible embarrassment. One day his best friend invited him to a sleepover with more of his very good friends and my son very much wanted to attend. He came to me crying and asked my opinion about the possibility of him going. He asked if I could think of anything that could help him attend without being embarrassed by a possible wet sleeping bag in the morning. I suggested a couple of things.

I agreed with him that he should go, I advised him to refrain from drinking any liquids from the time that he arrived until breakfast. I also suggested that he get dressed or undressed in the bathroom and I would send extra Pull-Ups along.

We then talked about having courage. I prayed with him and asked God to help him have the courage that he needed to take the first step to enjoy the time with his friends. He then prayed for himself. It was heart warming. He asked God to give him courage every minute.

When he returned, he said he had the best time he ever had in his whole life, and yes, he had an accident overnight but his buddies couldn't tell. That event gave him the courage to attend many other functions.

He now had a history with God.

*The deepest spiritual lessons are not learned
by His letting us have our way in the end,
but by His making us wait, bearing with us in love
and patience until we are able to honestly pray
what He taught his disciples to pray. Thy will be done.*
ELISABETH ELLIOT

Teaching Our Children to Wait

Living in a   society where we want everything quickly, I think it is important to teach our children what it means to wait. Waiting is not something that comes easily to people, especially children, but the Bible tells us how important it is to learn to wait for the Lord.

Our children can quickly become impatient, stressed, unhappy, and frustrated when they are waiting for something. I found that it really was not that hard to teach them that there are benefits to learning to wait patiently.

There's an easier way.
Here are some tips:

1. Memorize scripture. Seven of my favorite verses that I used to teach my children how to wait include:

"I waited patiently for the Lord; He turned to me and heard my cry. He lifted me out of the slimy pit, out of the mud and mire. He set my feet on a rock and gave me a firm place to stand."
Psalm 40:1

"Wait for the Lord: be strong and take heart and wait for the Lord."
Psalm 27:14

"The Lord is my strength and my shield. He has heard my cry for mercy. My heart trusts in Him and I am helped."
Psalm 28:6-7

"Blessed are all those who wait for the Lord."
Isaiah 30:18

"But the fruit of the Spirit is love, joy, peace, patience, kindness, goodness, faithfulness, gentleness, and self-control. Against such things there is no law."
Galatians 5:22-23

2. Be a role model in front of our children. We can be in a hurry and yet not be impatient or stressed. Finding ourselves in a situation where we are forced to slow down does not have to cause us to become impatient or angry. Whether it is potty training our child, or teaching them to tie their shoes, or finding ourselves in a traffic jam, or any number of every day life events, we can be the role models for our children.

3. Affirm the child when they are waiting patiently. Affirm them when they are waiting patiently while playing with their sibling, or while in a restaurant waiting for food, or any other circumstance. Be on the lookout for opportunities to complement them when they are improving their ability to wait patiently.

Be patient. Do the best with what you know.
When you know more, adjust the trajectory.
JEN HATMAKER

Dealing with Disappointment

hat should we say to our children when they whine and complain and say that life is not fair?

It is important to help our children understand the Bible clearly says that in this life we will have trouble.

"In this world you will have trouble but take heart,
I have overcome the world."
John 16:33

When asked in Matthew chapter 18 how many times we need to forgive others, Jesus replied 70x7. That means that the chances of us being hurt, and needing to forgive people in our lifetime will probably be very great. Being hurt can be a great source of disappointment.

In Luke chapter 17, we are told that we will have the opportunity to be offended. It states that offenses will come, but we should choose not to feel offended. Those instances also include opportunities to feel disappointment.

If we know then, that in this life we will have troubles, and we will be hurt and/or offended by other people, how do we teach our children to deal with it?

There's an easier way.

Here are some tips:

1. **Talk with your children about disappointments** because 'life isn't fair.' Discuss the impossibility of defining the word fair. Was it fair for God to send His Son to die for us on a cross?

Memorize scriptures that explain that the world does not revolve around them and their happiness. God created us to make a difference in the world and tell others about His love. Here are three of my favorites that we memorized.

"Then Jesus said to his disciples,
Whoever wants to be my disciple must deny
themselves and take up their cross and follow me.
For whoever wants to save their life will lose it,
but whoever loses their life for me
will find it."
Matthew 16:24-25

"I have been crucified with Christ
and I no longer live, but Christ lives in me.
The life I now live in the body,
I live by faith in the son of God,
who loved me and gave himself for me."
Galatians 2:20

2. Explain to your children that sometimes things just don't turn out the way we had hoped and planned. It is easy and natural to feel disappointed. It does not mean that we have done something wrong, or that it was not God's perfect plan. We can assume that it was God's plan A. We rarely see the bigger picture, and we know that God's ways are higher than our ways.

"We need to thank God IN every situation,
so when we feel disappointed
we thank Him and praise Him."
1 Thessalonians 5:16-18

3. Look for something we can learn from our disappointment. For example, let's say your child struck out several times during his weekly T-ball game. He was so disappointed. Maybe the problem was something he was doing, and it could be corrected.

A child that doesn't practice enough can have a disappointing recital. Disappointments of this kind can be great learning opportunities for the future.

4. **Accept the fact that sometimes the very plans that we feel have been thwarted were actually meant to benefit us** in a different way, or maybe even benefit someone else.

There have been times when we were given a revelation into how God was using our seemingly failed plans to benefit someone. Those have been faith building times. Other times we just chose to believe by faith that God had another idea.

I love Dr. Timothy Keller's quote, when comparing the prayer lives of our forefather Joseph in the book of Genesis and the prophet Elisha in the book of 2 Kings. From the accounts in the Bible, it appears that Joseph's prayers are not answered by God, but Elisha's prayers are answered immediately. Dr. Keller writes, "In Joseph's story we see that God does not give us exactly what we asked for. Instead He gives us what we would have asked for if we had known everything He knows."

So, even through our disappointments, we trust and thank God.

Motivating Your Children

We read in Proverbs 22 verse 15 that, "Foolishness is bound in the heart of a child. The rod of discipline will remove it far from him." Disciplining and training our children include many techniques and practices. One of my favorites is to motivate them to want to do what is right. If we can motivate our children to choose to do what is right because it is right, we have given them a crucial tool to use in filling their destinies.

There's an easier way.

Here are some tips:

1. The most important tip is to separate our love for them from their performance. They must understand that we will love them regardless of what they do or don't do. We will love them unconditionally, just as God loves us. However, as we teach, train, lead, and discipline them, we need to be careful that the love we show them does not change. It's important that they understand that.

2. Reward their character, even more than their performance. In the third chapter of first Corinthians we learn that not only is it important that we labor, but that we labor well. Our attitude and issues of the heart are just as important as the work we accomplish.

3. Motivate the children with verbal affirmation and encouragement. Be looking for ways to encourage them daily. We can say things like, "I love your smile and good attitude while you're accomplishing hard things." Or, "I am so glad that you're my helper, you bring joy to our family."

4. We need to be a good role model as we work throughout the day. We need to examine our tone of voice, and our attitude. Are we grumbling as we work? Do we do things well? Do we ask them for forgiveness when we have wronged them?

5. Affection is a great motivator. It's important throughout the day to show physical affection.

THERE'S AN EASIER WAY

6. Pray with your child for their day, and their attitude, and whatever else might be on their heart. It not only draws you together, but it motivates them to want to do better, knowing that God is involved in their life and their day.

You can give without loving,
but you cannot love without giving."
AMY CARMICHAEL

Finding Friends

T his chapter differs from the other chapters. The tips in this chapter are meant specifically for moms, although it will ultimately help children as well. It is important for every mom to have at least one really good friend. More than one is even better.

After I had my second child I felt so lonely. It was just too much work to take both boys out and socialize, and equally too much work to invite people into my home. So instead, I just grumbled and felt sorry for myself. I knew that a major part of my answer was to develop friendships with women.

It is not that my husband was not enough, it was just that he was not meant to meet all of my needs, and couldn't fully understand some of the issues that I was going through as a young mom of young children. *Women need women friends.* They not only help to support us, but they become an important part of your family's foundation. They pray for us and support us, as we go through the ups and downs of life.

In addition, young moms need older, more experienced moms as friends to mentor them. Those same young moms should be actively looking for someone they can mentor.

Before I had children I was socially active with six close girlfriends. We vacationed together, and spent almost every weekend together. We eventually all married and had children within 1 to 2 years of each other. Life just became too complicated and too busy for us to socialize anymore.

I knew something had to change.

There's an easier way.

Here are some tips.

1. **Pray.** Ask God to help you to reconnect with a friend, or to bring a new friend or friends into your life. Pray also for someone who could mentor you and someone that you could mentor.

2. **Decide what kind of social activities would benefit you.** Maybe a weekly MOPS group, or a monthly Bible study, or maybe even a group that you organize to get together on a regular, or as needed basis. These are all great ways to meet and connect with other moms.

The six pre-marriage girlfriends that I referenced earlier decided to get together once a month for breakfast.

From the time that we left our homes until we returned to our homes could not take more than one hour. We all had young children and very busy lives however, we all felt the need to reconnect our friendships. Most of us bartered babysitting with another family for that hour. I would babysit for a mom one hour a month, and she would return the favor for me. Years later we are still meeting as a group, just once a month for one hour. It's just enough time to share prayer requests and family news. It's wonderful. What would work for you?

3. **As you make arrangements to mentor someone, or meet with a mentor, decide the boundaries.** What works the best with your schedules? Would Skyping be effective? Would meeting once a month work for both of you, or how about emails or phone calls? Both of you probably lead very busy lives. Come up with a schedule, but be prepared to be flexible. Life as a mom has a way of changing without much notice.

4. **If you enjoy entertaining in your home but think that it's impossible, it's not.** If cleaning is the issue, just clean the rooms where the company will be spending their time. If even the thought of cleaning those rooms seems overwhelming, for desperate times, put everything that is out of place in a big black garbage bag, and store it in your bedroom until the party's over. Then, put the items away. I make a point to keep a very clean kitchen, dining area and bathroom. That's about it. You enter the other rooms at your own risk.

If the problem is you don't like to cook, you can have a potluck meal. I supply the drinks and all of the utensils and plates and cups, and my company provides the main food. Or, supply the drinks and dessert and let your company provide the rest of the food. Sometimes, I will invite company over just for coffee, tea, and dessert, which I often purchase, if time is an issue.

What would make you feel comfortable showing hospitality to your friends?

Make it work for you.

17

*Leave it all in the Hands
that were wounded for you.*
ELISABETH ELLIOT

The I statement

When my husband and I were dating we had the greatest relationship. After we were married much of what my husband did started to bother me. *Unfortunately, I handled it by yelling at him.* My first pregnancy, six months after our wedding, brought morning sickness and even more frustration and anger. One day while listening to Elisabeth Elliot on the radio I learned something that helped with my anger and became an important tool in raising our children.

There's an easier way.

Here are some tips:

I learned how to communicate using an 'I' statement. Learning to communicate with I statements made such a difference not only with my husband, but with our children.

It helped me to teach the children
how to communicate in a way
that reduced anger and frustration.

Over the years I've come to realize that I statements helped me significantly in two ways. The first, is that **it forced me to stop and think before I spoke.** For instance, if one of my children spilled a cup of milk, instead of just reacting in anger and saying something like, "Johnny that is the fourth time this week you spilled something. What could possibly be wrong with you?", I would take the time to figure out how to communicate what I was feeling without putting him on the defensive. *It helps the person I am talking to hear my heart and what I am dealing with and it gives them time to think about it also.*

The second result that I saw, was that during the time it took for me to formulate the I statement, **I could organize my thoughts and get to the root of what was causing my anger or frustration.** Maybe, I was so exhausted, the problem was my attitude, and not the action of the other person at all that was bothering me.

Elisabeth Elliot explained that the I statement had three parts. The first part is 'I feel'. So I am stating the feeling. For instance, I feel angry. I feel sad. I feel frustrated, or confused, unappreciated, worried, anxious, or hurt, etc. It is important NOT to say 'I feel like.' The second part is 'when you.' So far we have, I feel, when you. When you what? What behavior are you talking about? The third part is 'because.' Because describes why you feel the way that you do. So, we have—

"I feel _____ when you ____ because ____."

I find that this way to communicate works best with children ages five or six and older. It works very well with adults also. Children under five do not really have the ability to reason things out and understand the I statement.

Example #1. If your child walks in with muddy shoes on your newly mopped floor, knowing that they are to take their shoes off before coming into the house, you could say, "I feel frustrated when you make the floor dirty because I've just washed it and you know the rule about taking shoes off before coming into the house."

Example #2. Your six-year-old leaves his art supplies out all over the table and even leaves the paint and glue uncapped. "I feel disappointed when you leave your art supplies all over the table because you know that when you are finished working on a project everything must be put away."

Example #3. Your child has promised to help you with the chores, but when it is time to do the work he is outside playing and has forgotten all about it. The I statement could be: "I feel sad when you don't keep your promise to help me with the chores because I trusted your word, and it took me longer than I had planned since I was working alone."

The I statements do not take the place of discipline. If my child leaves the art supplies out again after explaining to them why it is wrong, I would probably discipline the child. **I statements help us to explain what we are feeling without causing defensiveness or anger,** or a misunderstanding between two people.

Elisabeth Elliot gave the example of a young woman married for less than a year who was having trouble dealing with her often angry husband. The young woman finally used an I statement with her husband. She said, "Honey, I feel intimidated when you shout because I feel unappreciated and unloved." And to the amazement of even Elisabeth Elliot, her husband stopped yelling at her. He had no idea how his shouting was affecting her. It was just the way his father had talked to his mother.

I started this chapter by describing the turmoil in the first year of my marriage. One of the things that my husband and I fought most about was what happened at our kitchen table. I was raised in a family that celebrated meal times together. At breakfast and supper we enjoyed hearty conversation and laughter. My husband, however, was raised in a family that read individually at the table during each meal. So his father would read the newspaper, his mom might be reading a magazine or the mail, and each child just sat at the table reading whatever was available.

Our first meal as a married couple surprised me when my husband reached for the newspaper and then read it silently right in front of me. *I was furious.* We fought many times over table etiquette.

Then I learned the I statement technique. I quietly and respectfully said to my husband, "I feel disrespected and unloved when you read at the table because I was not raised that way." He looked at me with respect and said he was glad to finally understand why I would get so upset when he would be reading. We came to an agreement that day as to what would happen at our table for mealtimes. After a year of fighting the whole problem was taken care of with one I statement.

When you feel yourself starting to get upset, stop and use an I statement.

It has been wonderful to see my children grow up and use I statements. Recently, one of my daughters approached me and asked if she could speak with me. She said, "Mom, I need to talk to you. I feel hurt, and angry, when you remind me to do things because I am not a little girl anymore."

Speaking with I statements leaves no room for arguments. We hear what is said, how the person feels and why they feel that way. It then becomes our choice as to whether or not we make a difference in our behavior.

Learning to use I statements and teaching our children to do the same, becomes an important tool to help them communicate effectively.

A happy marriage is the union of two good forgivers.
RUTH BELL GRAHAM

Have a Better Marriage

*A*s you discovered in the last chapter, at the beginning of our marriage, I was not the kind of person ANYONE would want for a wife. I was sarcastic, selfish, and pessimistic. My dear husband put up with a lot during the first year of our marriage. I had an epiphany when our first child, a son, was born. My eyes were opened. I repented. I asked God and my husband to forgive me, and I have been learning and applying what I have learned to my marriage since that day.

There's an easier way.

Here are some tips to have a better marriage:

1. **Be KIND.** As I stated earlier, my eyes were opened when our son was born. The very second he was born,

my first thought was that if he were to marry, I never wanted his future wife to treat him the way I was treating his father. *My husband was someone's son.* He was created in the image of God and no one deserved my behavior. I needed to talk to my husband with respect, see him with God's eyes and treat him with unconditional love.

2. **Educate yourself.** Men and women handle life, stress, and problems differently. Listen to podcasts, read books, and/or attend a marriage conference to help you better understand your mate. Ask each other frequently what could be done to improve the marriage. *Open communication is vital for two people to become one.*

3. **Study biblical submission.** Discuss your findings with your hubby. Make sure that you understand each other. *Pray for each other daily.*

4. **Go back to the basics.** Is marriage 50/50 or is it 100/100? Your marriage is the one that your children will emulate. It is the only normal that your children know. Would you be pleased if your child's marriage is just like yours? If not, make some changes. There is a bigger picture. God created the idea of marriage. *Seeking God and getting to know His character, will help you love your mate unconditionally.*

5. **Try your best to have daily devotions, preferably WITH your husband.** Find a reading plan or devotional

that will work for you, and try to read the Bible every day, even if it's for several minutes. I find that I tend to sense God's voice and direction when I take the time to be quiet and read His word. *The more I 'hear' from God, the more I am able to look at my husband the way that God sees him.*

6. **Have a girlfriend in whom you can confide.** Most husbands do not want to hear about all of the drama in our life. When confiding, we need be very careful not to talk about our husbands or gossip about anyone. *Sometimes we just need a human sounding board who will give us honest feedback, and support us in prayer.*

19

Take the world but give me Jesus;
in His cross my trust will be,
till, with clear, brighter vision,
face to face my Lord I see.
FANNY CROSBY

Trusting God

pproximately seven years ago one of my children was diagnosed with a very serious health issue. As he and I sat in the doctors office listening to the bad report, I remember thinking how wrong I was. For years I had assumed that I was pretty much in control of everything that had happened and would happen to my children. How naïve and ignorant I was.

When they were young it was easy to control what they ate and what they wore and who they were with and what occupied their time. Even as they got older I largely determined what happened in their life.

Now one of my children was facing a life-changing illness and future surgeries, and I couldn't change it and I couldn't fix it.

That realization started me on a journey that is continuing today. Can I trust God with my life and the lives of my children? What does trusting God look like? What does it feel like? What should I do when it's hard? How should I react in troubled times? Are hard times in my children's lives my fault? Could I have prayed more effectively, or more often? Was it faulty prayers on my part?

I researched every verse in the Bible that used the word trust. I wrote them all down and asked God to help me understand what it means to trust Him. I am definitely still a work in progress, however, I am learning more and more how to trust God.

There's an easier way.

Here are some tips:

1. **Do not be surprised when troubles come.** The Bible clearly states that we will have trouble in this world,

> "I have told you these things so that in
> me you may have peace. In this world
> you will have trouble. But take heart I
> have overcome the world."
> *John 16:33.*

So when there are troubles, I should not be surprised. I should understand that in this world there will be ups and downs and I need to learn how to react to both good times and hard times. *I am not to feel guilty when trouble comes. It does not mean that I caused it, or prayed ineffectively.*

2. **Do not project.** Just because I can not see what I hope will happen, or I can not figure out how a situation could end well, does not mean that it can't or won't. I am not to base my thoughts about the future on regrets that I have had in the past, or fears that torment me now. I need to have a steadfast heart.

"Trust in the Lord with all your heart and lean not on your own understanding; in all your ways acknowledge Him and He will make your paths straight."
Proverbs 3:5-6

"You will keep in perfect peace him whose mind is steadfast, because he trusts in you."
Isaiah 26:3

3. **Be of good courage and learn to wait.**

"Wait for the Lord, be strong and take heart and wait for the Lord."
Psalm 27:14

Although I would prefer instant fixes to my problems, that is generally not the way it works in the faith realm. I must learn that God's timing may not be my timing. However, His plan is always best. There is never a good time to give up hope.

"I will trust God forever."
Psalm 52:8

4. God does not need my power to make things work. When I am weak, God is strong.

"My grace is sufficient for you,
for My power is made perfect in weakness."
2 Corinthians 12:9

It does not take strength to have trust in God, it takes faith. It is not weakness to trust God, it is obedience.

"Those who know your name will trust in you."
Psalm 9:10

5. My ability to trust God is proportionate to my understanding of His character, and His love for me. The more I read the Bible and learn about Him, the easier it is for me to trust Him with my life, the life of my children, and my prayer concerns.

20

Never eat more than you can lift.
MISS PIGGY

The Twenty-Meal Plan

J am not sure why it surprised me day after day to realize that I had to make supper for my family. Who did I think was going to make it, or why did I think that this day would be different than any other day? I do not enjoy cooking in the first place, and I was getting tired of my daily 4:00 PM panic. I made a change. I first tried freezer cooking. Then, I made 30 meals in 1 day. When that did not work, I made supper before I made breakfast. Finally, I tried making two meals a day, (one to eat and one to freeze). **But none of those great ideas worked for me!**

After several other attempts to stay on top of meal planning, I came up with a system that worked so well that I used it for more than ten years!

There's an easier way.

Here are some tips that made meal planning easier for me:

1. **Have a basic plan.** The simplest plan is better than no plan. Ideas that don't work are just part of the journey to illuminate the one that will. Even if I loved to cook, I still think that it would take some planning and effort to have stress-free meals. My 10-year meal plan consisted of making a list of our twenty favorite meals and serving them weekdays, every month.

> **Every month we eat
> the same 20 suppers.**

It saved me time and money. If an ingredient that I knew I would use was on sale, I bought a large quantity. Weekends, I tried to make more creative meals. For breakfast, I alternated oatmeal, pancakes, and eggs. Lunches were leftovers from the refrigerator or pantry.

This particular plan may not work for you, but if you struggle with meal planning, hopefully one or more of these tips will help.

2. **Keep the atmosphere in the house pleasant.** Meals are an integral part of making a house a loving home and moms typically determine the mood in that home. *Panicking every day around 4:00 PM and grumbling day after day about making meals was not creating a pleasant atmosphere in my home.* Using the 20 meal plan, plastering a smile on my face, playing inspirational CDs

while cooking, and lighting a candle in the kitchen—all of these changed the mood in our home.

3. **Have all of the ingredients needed to cook an emergency supper.** It should be one that doesn't take a lot of effort, just in case your day is out of control. I always keep 3-4 cans of New England Clam Chowder in the pantry in case of an emergency.

I also use leftover vegetables, noodles, and meats from Monday through Thursday to make a soup to eat on Friday. It's easy, healthy, and economical. If there aren't enough leftovers, I freeze what I do have for another week. *Is there something you could make regularly to make mealtime easier?*

4. **Keep mealtimes themselves pleasant.** It is NOT a good time for a battle. I refused to allow my children to whine and complain at the table about the meal that they were served. I wanted the time to be filled with laughter and love. Small children were served small portions. They were expected to try everything on their plate. They could have more, but if they didn't finish what was on their plate they had to wait until the next meal or snack time to eat again. We didn't spend time arguing about food. *What would work to keep mealtime pleasant at your house?*

5. **Make food fun by serving it in different forms, AND have the children help to make it happen.** Use a dehydrator to dry bananas or tomatoes or strawberries, or

freeze fruits and use them in smoothies or in yogurt. The children can arrange the food on the trays or shelves for the freezer or the dehydrator. We also learned to eat a lot of raw vegetables with a healthy dip. The children can arrange the vegetables on plates for snack times or meals.

6. **Eat healthy food.** If you know that there are ways that you could be serving more healthy foods, take baby steps to help it happen. When I researched the adverse effects of white flour on our digestive system, I decided my first step would be to stop buying white bread. I didn't cut out all white flour because it was just too traumatic and overwhelming. Eventually over a year, I cut out as much white flour AND sugar that I could. Baby step by baby step I cut out desserts and sweetened drinks from our diets. It took several years. *What would work for you?*

7. **Involve your children in setting, decorating, and clearing the table.** Children LOVE to help, and especially enjoy creating a centerpiece for the table. Duplos, Legos, stuffed animals, Hess trucks, dolls, flowering weeds, snake skins, and many other treasures have graced the center of our table to the pleasure and pride of the creator.

We have this one life to offer;
there is no second chance.
JEN HATMAKER

Capturing Memories

*D*o you take hundreds of pictures with your phone, tablet and camera, and then wish they would magically appear organized and immortalized in beautiful scrapbooks?

Would you love an organized way to remember all of the wonderful things that our young children are saying and doing?

Do you feel overwhelmed by planning birthday parties and other events?

There's an easier way.

Here are some tips:

1. **Just do it.** Make a decision to do SOMETHING with your photos. I randomly decided that each December, I would use Shutterfly, to make a photo album for each

of my children, and one for me. As soon as the albums are delivered, I delete every picture from my camera and computer.

Maybe you would prefer to create scrapbooks. I made scrapbooks for my first four children by snatching time every Saturday morning. I kept all of the supplies in a crate, and on Saturday mornings, I pulled it out and as quickly as I could, I would create 1-2 pages at a time. Not magazine worthy, but done.

I stopped scrapbooking when I started ordering from Shutterfly.

2. **Take fewer, but more meaningful photos.** I do not take more than 3-4 pictures of each child during a special event. I felt so guilty deleting adorable pictures of my even more adorable children, that I learned to put more thought into the pictures I took.

3. **Look for new ways that technology can do the work for you.** Recently, I have been very intentional with my photos on Instagram. I use a program called Chat Books, which organizes 60 consecutive pictures with their captions from my Instagram account. It prints them, binds them in a small book, and ships it to me automatically. I am notified as soon as I have posted 60 pictures, and I can choose to delete or change the pictures or captions before the book is sent to me.

4. **Have a plan for all of the arts and crafts that your children create.** I take pictures of the artwork created by

my children and make a photo album for each child with the photos. The artwork is then thrown away. I only save 3-4 pieces of artwork for each child. As they move out of our home, I hand them their artwork.

5. **Save their adorable sayings in an easily organized system.** I realized quickly after my second child that I would never remember all of the adorable things that my children said. So, I decided that I would write cute words and sayings on a calendar. At the end of the year, I would gather the information, organize it by child, and put it in individual folders. Their folder held important medical and dental records, school report cards, and other 'official' papers. As they move out, their folders go with them.

6. **Plan backwards for special occasions.** Think about your goals. At the end of the birthday celebration, or the holiday, what will you have hoped to achieve? How do you want your loved ones to feel? Combine those goals with your personality.

When I plan, food is my lowest priority. I just don't enjoy working with food. I use the same menu for Christmas Day every year. I use the same menu for Easter every year. For birthday celebrations we eat Chinese food. I put more of my efforts into decorations, planning games, and purchasing special gifts. What works with your personality?

Also, there are no rules stating that you have to have large celebrations for birthdays every year. Create a plan, and feel free to change your mind. I have a group of friends who choose to celebrate their children's 1st, 5th, 10th, 16th and 21st birthdays with extended family members. Other birthdays have smaller celebrations.

Remember, YOU have ownership over celebrations. No one knows how your loved ones will feel cherished as well as you do.

Make family memories
according to the heartbeat
of YOUR family.

Our prayer and hope
is that the tips in this book
will inspire you and bless you
as you raise your children for His glory.
We would love to hear from you!

BONNI GREINER

Books
Recapturing the Joy of Motherhood
Timely Truths for Toddlers to Tweens

Social Media
Blog: www.mombyexample.com
Facebook: www.facebook.com/mombyexample

KATHY MCCCLURE

Chalkboard Word Art
(FREE downloads at frugallancaster.com/downloads)
God Has Given You by Sally Clarkson
You are Loved (Romans 5:8)

Social Media
Blog: www.frugallancaster.com
Facebook: www.facebook.com/frugallancasterpa
Twitter: www.twitter.com/frugallancaster
Pinterest: www.pinterest.com/frugallancaster

Made in the USA
Lexington, KY
12 July 2017